William Walton
A Clarinet Album

Arranged by
Christopher Palmer

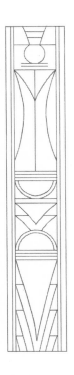
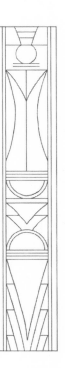

CONTENTS

Music Department
OXFORD UNIVERSITY PRESS
Oxford and New York

Oxford University Press, Walton Street, Oxford OX2 6DP, England
Oxford University Press, 200 Madison Avenue, New York, NY 10016, USA

Oxford is a trade mark of Oxford University Press

© Oxford University Press 1992

Seven Pieces from Façade

1. Popular Song

Printed in Great Britain

OXFORD UNIVERSITY PRESS, MUSIC DEPARTMENT, WALTON STREET, OXFORD OX2 6DP

2. Scotch Rhapsody

William Walton
A Clarinet Album

Arranged by
Christopher Palmer

Music Department
OXFORD UNIVERSITY PRESS
Oxford and New York

Seven Pieces from Façade

1. Popular Song

Clarinet in B♭

2. Scotch Rhapsody

3. Polka

4. Something Lies Beyond the Scene

5. Tango-Pasodoble

6. Fox-trot
'Old Sir Faulk'

7. March

(from *Façade II*)

8. Romanza

(from *Christopher Columbus*)

9. Three Pieces from The First Shoot

I

(Waltz)

II

III
(Envoi)

3. Polka

11

4. Something Lies Beyond the Scene

14

5. Tango-Pasodoble

6. Fox-trot
'Old Sir Faulk'

7. March

(from *Façade II*)

8. Romanza

(from *Christopher Columbus*)

9. Three Pieces from The First Shoot

I

(Waltz)

II

III
(Envoi)